Interviews

24
Paula Errando
Indie Fashion Advocate

29
Jasmin Waschl
Guardian of Underground Art

33
Poe de Laf
Wrap It Up

50
Toni Varela
No Rules, No Limits

58
Albert Adrià
Beyond elBulli

66
Meritxell Falgueras
Breaking the Wine Glass Ceiling

Showcase

38
Spain's First Influencers
Bocaccio & the Gauche Divine

Story

74
The Porter

Photo: Alin Gavriliuc

Barcelona. You picture Gaudí, crowded beaches and familiar plazas. But that's just the surface. Locals know a different city: the skateboarding capital of Europe, a vanguard of food and drink, an art scene with graffiti outlaws and manipulated media.

LOST iN is your inside track to the secrets so tightly guarded by locals. You'll meet the fifth-generation wine celebrity paving the way for female sommeliers. The stage director who built an indie fashion hub. The nightclub that liberated the city. The chef who saved his family restaurant by risking it all.

Along the way, you'll step inside a culture of secret speakeasies, surrealist dance parties, hidden restaurants and a festival that literally sets the streets on fire. We'll even peek inside the city's most surprising design statement: wildly theatrical bathrooms. One even doubles as a disco.

This is Mediterranean magic unlocked by the locals who make it happen. Get lost in the real Barcelona that most people will never know.

1
Editorial

4
The Giradabo

6
Top Five

8
Neighborhoods

14
Outdoors

18
Gather

22
Shops

26
Art & Design

34
Bespoke Bathrooms

48
Bites

60
Sips

62
Speakeasies

70
Day Trip
A Roman Holiday in Spain

72
Editors' Picks

As your gondola ascends, Barcelona unfolds beneath you like a living map: the Mediterranean glittering to the east, Eixample's geometric grid laid out below and city sprawl extending in every direction. At the top, you're suspended 1,800 feet above sea level, taking in a 360-degree panorama. The Giradabo Ferris wheel is a 2014 addition to Europe's highest amusement park atop Tibidabo mountain. This is peak Barcelona.

• Giradabo, Pl. del Tibidabo, 3, 4, Sarrià-Sant Gervasi, tibidabo.cat

Photo: Nikola Tasic

Top Five

You want the best, you got the best.

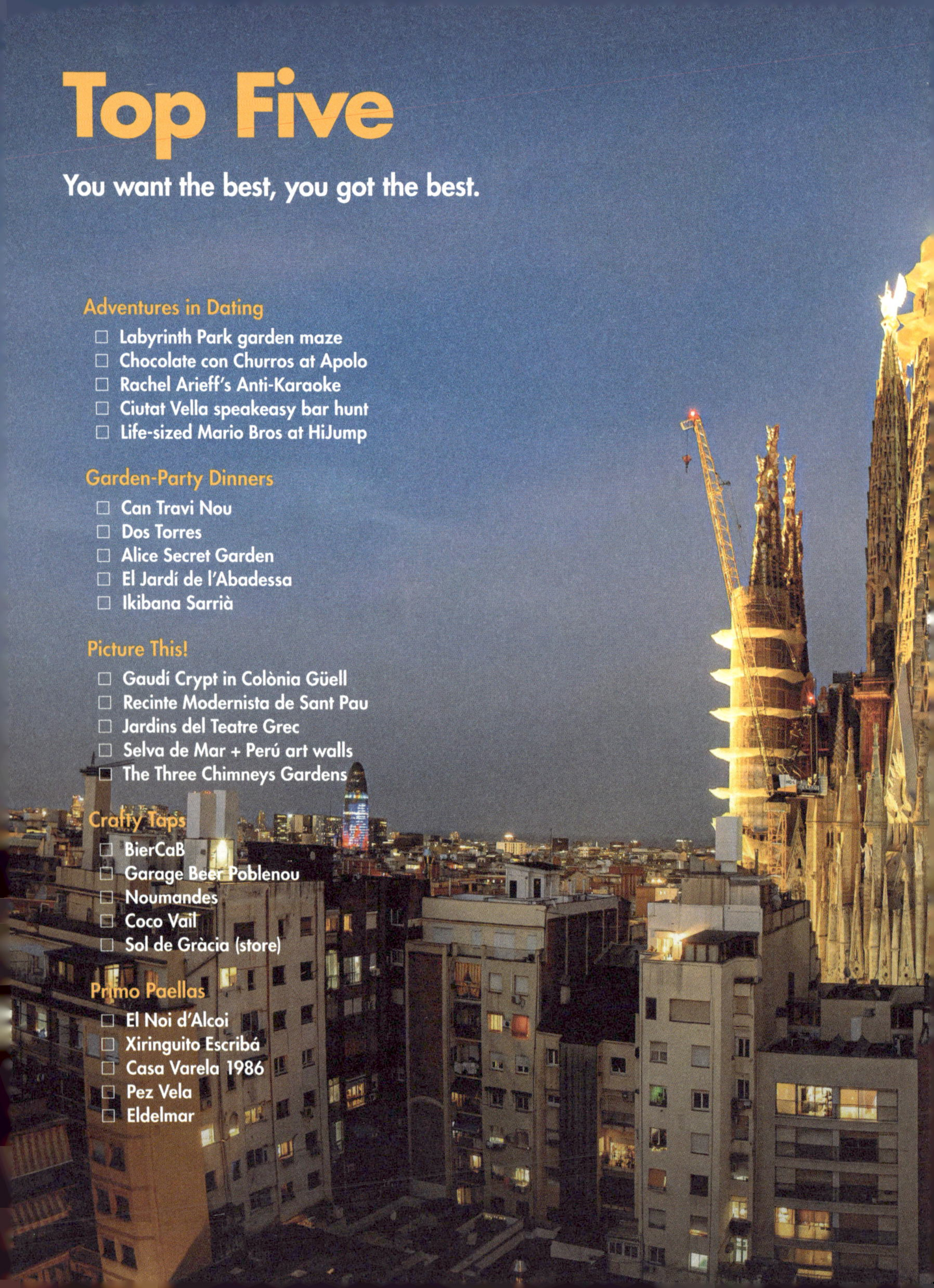

Adventures in Dating

- ☐ Labyrinth Park garden maze
- ☐ Chocolate con Churros at Apolo
- ☐ Rachel Arieff's Anti-Karaoke
- ☐ Ciutat Vella speakeasy bar hunt
- ☐ Life-sized Mario Bros at HiJump

Garden-Party Dinners

- ☐ Can Travi Nou
- ☐ Dos Torres
- ☐ Alice Secret Garden
- ☐ El Jardí de l'Abadessa
- ☐ Ikibana Sarrià

Picture This!

- ☐ Gaudí Crypt in Colònia Güell
- ☐ Recinte Modernista de Sant Pau
- ☐ Jardins del Teatre Grec
- ☐ Selva de Mar + Perú art walls
- ☐ The Three Chimneys Gardens

Crafty Taps

- ☐ BierCaB
- ☐ Garage Beer Poblenou
- ☐ Noumandes
- ☐ Coco Vail
- ☐ Sol de Gràcia (store)

Primo Paellas

- ☐ El Noi d'Alcoi
- ☐ Xiringuito Escribà
- ☐ Casa Varela 1986
- ☐ Pez Vela
- ☐ Eldelmar

Photo: Christopher Politano

Neighborhoods

Barrios de Barcelona

Past & Present

History collides with modern culture in a maze of crooked lanes and stone facades. That's the enduring allure of Ciutat Vella (Old City), home to Barcelona's earliest neighborhoods.

It begins in El Born, once a stage for medieval jousts, now a retail battlefield of boutique fashion and timeless bodegas. The trendy quarter borders *Ciutadella Park* and its iconic *Monumental Waterfall*. Just south lies the Barri Gòtic (Gothic Quarter), built atop Roman ruins, where labyrinthine lanes open up into sunlit plazas. La Rambla, the city's most famous street, traces the line of an ancient riverbed and defensive wall, dividing the Gothic Quarter from El Raval. The latter, taking its name from the Arabic word for "suburb," continues south as a defiant, multicultural neighborhood. Despite its seedy past and the need for vigilance after dark, El Raval remains loaded with raw, underground art and culture. Finally, the city meets the sea at Barceloneta. Most of the neighborhood sits on land reclaimed from the water in the 18th century. The onetime fishing village stays true to its maritime roots with off-the-boat seafood and beaches that are lively, if not always pristine.

Ciutat Vella may be easier on the wallet, but it often exacts its price in other ways: pickpockets, late-night revelers and crowds that overwhelm its narrow streets. Even so, dismiss its subtle charms at your peril.

• Ciutat Vella

Photos: Mau Cardoso, Armin Pfarr

Photo: oidonnyboy

Gaudí on the Grid

Imagine 19th-century Barcelona, its entire population packed within the walls of Ciutat Vella. The city was bursting at the seams and in desperate need of an *eixample*, the Catalan word for "expansion." The urban plan that followed was visionary: a precise grid of octagonal blocks designed to give every resident equal access to light, air and quality of life. This is the defining face of Eixample, a district that feels like an open-air tribute to Art Nouveau. Within this grid of elegance, you'll find the city's highest concentration of Michelin-starred dining, flanked by legacy fashion houses and Antoni Gaudí masterpieces like *Sagrada Família, Casa Batlló* and *Casa Milà*. Eixample is neatly divided by Carrer de Balmes. To the east, the Dreta de l'Eixample (Right Eixample) projects luxury with the promenades of Passeig de Gràcia and Rambla de Catalunya. To the west, the Esquerra de l'Eixample (Left Eixample) offers a counterpoint, humming with youthful energy around the *University of Barcelona* and the LGBTQ+ enclave affectionately known as Gaixample.

• Eixample

Bohemian Heights

Perched above Eixample on the rising hillside, Gràcia has always retained the spirit of an independent village, even after being absorbed into the city in 1897. The neighborhood had its "Williamsburg moment" in the 2010s when artists, musicians and designers flocked here for its creative buzz and (then) affordable rents. Today, Gràcia thrives as a haven of boutiques, craft studios and local markets, where lively plazas like Plaça del Sol and Plaça de la Virreina double as outdoor living rooms for the city's youth. Gaudí left his mark here, too. His influence begins with the colorful *Casa Vicens* (photo), his first residential commission, and culminates at *Park Güell,* a mosaic garden where color spills across the stone and the city unfurls below.

• Gràcia

Photo: Federico Giampieri

Paint, Code, Swim, Repeat

Once the industrial heart of the northeast, Poblenou earned the nickname Catalan Manchester, a nod to England's manufacturing powerhouse. When factories and warehouses fell silent during postindustrial decline, they left behind an urban shell ripe for reinvention. Poblenou means "New Village," which is ironic since that's precisely what came next. Artists moved into the void, turning empty buildings into studios and blank walls into one of the city's earliest graffiti scenes. Next, a citywide facelift ahead of the 1992 Olympics developed the local beaches and brought new construction. An innovation plan in 2000 helped finish the transition, providing infrastructure and incentives for high-tech companies. The *new* New Village was now Barcelona's Silicon Valley, a name likely hatched in a marketing meeting. The Rambla del Poblenou has anchored the district as its main commercial artery for more than a century, but for a taste of its true character, duck onto the side streets. Here, sleek new shops and eateries share the pavement with the old legends that never left, and art bursts from every corner with modern galleries and museums standing beside street art and graffiti. And when the heat is on, you're just a short walk to Barcelona's best urban beaches.

• Poblenou

Photo: Aleksandar Pasaric

Around the Center

The tension between village tradition and modern ambition builds as you move beyond the city center. Just south, the working-class streets of Poble Sec are evolving with street art, skate parks, theaters and the pincho bars that line Carrer de Blai. Above it, *Montjuïc Park* offers quiet trails, historic castles, Olympic sites and views that stretch from the port to the mountains. Sants mirrors this shift, with art and skate culture flourishing around its namesake train station. L'Hospitalet de Llobregat, a separate city wedged between Barcelona and the airport, quietly hides an underground art scene between the rows of glass business towers. The affluent Zona Alta, an informal name for a set of neighborhoods on the hillside, unexpectedly hosts one of the top indie fashion pop-ups (*BCN en las Alturas*) in its historic Torre Bellesguard. Nearby, Les Corts blends university life with the iconic energy of the newly reopened *Camp Nou* stadium, home to FC Barcelona.

Northwest of the center, Sant Andreu is a former industrial hub getting second looks with new construction and *Nau Bostik*, a graffiti-covered space hosting artist residencies, vintage markets and Mash Fest, Spain's premier craft beer event founded by local faves Garage Beer. Further north, the steep slopes of Horta-Guinardó hide historic treasures like the Laberint d'Horta park and provide elevated views rarely seen by visitors. Moving east along the coast just past the city line, Sant Adrià de Besòs is shedding its industrial skin as street art collectives and alternative music festivals breathe new life into its riverfront and *Fòrum*-adjacent beaches. Its coastal neighbor, Badalona, offers an easy beach escape with Roman ruins and the Pont del Petroli, a long pier ideal for sunrise walks above the Mediterranean.

• Poble Sec & beyond

Hit the Deck

Barcelona, Europe's skate capital, is an urban playground with marble plazas and buttery downhill lines. Graffiti-covered parks like *Picnic DIY, Mar Bella* and *Pumptrack Paral·lel* are professionally designed, but the must-ride spots are unofficial: the benches outside Sants train station and the plaza at the *Museum of Contemporary Art of Barcelona (MACBA)*. A new expansion could eventually spoil the MACBA party, so hit that long granite ledge while it lasts. For the latest intel, drop into local shops like *Venero* and *Hey Ho, Amigos*.

• Various locations

Outdoors

Sol to Soul

In a dense city like Barcelona, outdoor space is currency. Spend it well.

Photos: Alina Bordunova, Ben Allan, Pere López Brosa licensed under CC BY-SA 3.0

City Hike

High in the Collserola mountains, the six-mile Carretera de les Aigües offers a scenic urban escape along a former water-pipe service road. Known as the Balcony of Barcelona, the path delivers a sweeping look at the entire city, from the spires of the Sagrada Família to the curve of the Mediterranean Sea. Reaching nearly 1,500 feet at its peak, the relatively flat terrain makes it ideal for a gentle hike, a steady run or an easy cycle. To access the fresh mountain air and panoramic city views, take the Vallvidrera Funicular. This inclined railway begins its steep climb from the Peu del Funicular station, located just off Avinguda de Vallvidrera in the upper Sarrià neighborhood.

• Carretera de les Aigües, access at Peu del Funicular, Sarrià

Pool Party

You don't need a hotel key to enjoy what's arguably the best pool in the Barcelona area. Opened on the sands of Gavà Mar in 2022, *Playa Grande* is a 13-room boutique hotel that caters exclusively to adults (16+) from May to October. For a posh pool day and access to a quieter stretch of beach, simply rent a sunbed and claim your all-day pass to this seaside retreat. Non-guests are also welcome for lunch at the sunny *Terrace* restaurant.

• Playa Grande, Carrer dels Tellinaires 17, Gavà, playagrande.cat

Photo: Playa Grande

Beach Day

Few big European cities can match Barcelona's direct access to the Mediterranean, though even its best city beaches are great only by city standards. For the real deal, head about 80 minutes north on the 2 bus to *Platja Gran* in Tossa de Mar. Picture golden sand beneath your feet, the azure Costa Brava waters ahead and the 12th-century *Vila Vella* fortress rising behind you. For lunch, wander up the cobbled lanes for a seafood *cim i tomba* stew and a chilled glass of cava. Locals typically skip the city beaches in favor of cozy coastal spots like this.

• Platja Gran, Tossa de Mar, Girona

Photos: Boris Hadjur, Polina Kocheva

Pools & Waterfalls

Day trips aren't just for beaches. Girona also rewards the effort of a bus-train combo with stunning hiking trails. In summer, the 5.5-mile *Ruta dels 7 Gorgs* unfolds like a fantasy, where a mountain torrent has carved seven turquoise pools and cascading waterfalls. Here, the hike is just the prelude to bliss. Each plunge into the emerald water feels like a private spa deep in the pre-Pyrenean forest. Do you dream of sharing these pools with a herd of humans? Of course not. That's why entry numbers are capped, and you'll need to book your pass in advance.

• Parking Font del Querol, GI-401, km. 3, Campdevànol, Girona

Sound Waves

Barcelona hits peak volume each year with two of Europe's most influential music festivals. Kicking off in late spring, Primavera Sound showcases indie rock, pop and genre-defying sounds with highly curated lineups (photo, with Idles). A few weeks later comes Sónar, a celebration of electronic music and digital culture. Sónar by Day and Sónar+D focus on creativity and technology, while Sónar by Night makes the dance floors bounce 'til dawn. "I think Sónar has put Barcelona in the center of the electronic culture map," says Georgia Taglietti, one of the festival's original organizers. "It helped build the cultural tourism that a city needs in order to be seen not only as a sightseeing spot, but as a cultural incubator."

• Several locations, primaverasound.com, sonar.es

Gather

Share the Moment

Too much happens in Barcelona to be a spectator. Get into the mix.

Night Lights

For three radiant nights each February, LLUM BCN transforms Poblenou into an open-air gallery of light and imagination. This free festival fuses art, technology and architecture through installations and large-scale projections by renowned artists and emerging design students. The industrial grid becomes a sprawling, walkable stage for these high-tech creations. With contributors using tools like AI, VR and interactive mapping, LLUM casts Poblenou's modern towers and old factory walls in a kaleidoscope of color and glow. Grab a hot chocolate and prepare to wander, as the streets themselves become part of the exhibition.

• Several locations, Poblenou, @llumbcn

Arkham Unchained

From Halloween blowouts at Dracula's Castle in Romania to pop surrealist parties inspired by Okuda San Miguel and Ron English, Elrow turns every venue into a riot of color and chaos. Think confetti cannons, giant inflatables, acrobats, actors and an army of costumed performers, all set to high-energy electronic beats. Each event is built around an immersive theme, from a psychedelic trip through the jungle to an undersea adventure with pirates and mermaids. The music selection favors house and techno, providing a driving soundtrack to visual spectacles that overwhelm the senses. Founded in Barcelona in 2010, the company's global rise has made local appearances less common, but homecomings still happen at least twice a year, with OFFSónar among the regular highlights.

• Several locations, elrow.com

Run Like Hell

Few experiences scare the crap out of tourists like correfoc, a "fire run" that turns the streets of Catalonia into a blazing inferno. Dressed as devils and wielding pitchforks, participants dance down the street to the beat of tabal drummers while fireworks and scepters shower the city in pyrotechnics. The tradition traces back to medieval Devils' Dances, but the modern correfoc started spontaneously in 1978 when a group of locals quite literally lit up Barcelona. It soon became a staple of La Mercè (September) and other neighborhood festivals. Officially, the correfoc honors Catalan identity and revives traditions once banned under Franco. Unofficially, it revels in joyful defiance and the freedom to be wild and rebellious in public spaces.

Photos: Adrià Masi, Ramon Perucho, flydime, Festa Major del Clot,

High Society

Barcelona doesn't have cannabis shops but *social clubs*, private associations where members can buy and consume on site. The law lives in a gray zone. Officially, membership is limited to residents invited by an existing member, making it off-limits to tourists. In practice, some clubs quietly admit visitors with foreign passports (yes, we tested this). The usual process starts online, where you request an invitation. Conversations about specifics are never handled by phone or email, and once you're inside, let the staff lead the way. Bring a government-issued ID and cash (typically €20 to €50) for the membership fee. Most importantly, steer clear of street promoters, as they're often tied to scams or illegal operations

• Several locations

Shops

The Local Edit

Boutiques, markets and design shops where every purchase tells a story.

Read 'Em and Eat

Housed in a former Gothic-style chapel, *La Central Raval* is one of Barcelona's most atmospheric bookstores, with more than 70,000 titles on art, design and food as well as fiction in several languages. Wander through the shelves, then make your way to the heart of the store and discover one of Raval's hidden sanctuaries: a sun-drenched courtyard framed by palm trees and centuries-old stone. Settle in with a glass of vermouth and a toasted bikini sandwich, and lose yourself in a good read amid the calm and greenery. Can you take a book out here without buying it? Absolutely. Just handle it with care until you return it to the shelves.

• La Central Raval, Carrer d'Elisabets 6, El Raval, lacentral.com

Born This Way

Beyond the tourist glitter and Gaudí trinkets, El Born's medieval lanes hide one of Barcelona's more refined design scenes. For handcrafted leather, visit *Manuel Dreesmann* or *Iriarte Iriarte*. Step into *About Arianne* for modern women's footwear, or browse limited-edition accessories by Lucía Vergara at *Après Ski*. Feel the Mediterranean spirit in the homeware at *Bon Vent*, then slip into a *Natalie Capell* dress inside a space that channels Tim Burton fantasy. Finish your day treasure hunting for vintage gems at *The Room* and one-of-a-kind cover-ups and kimonos at *Mermaiding House*.

• Several locations, El Born

Vinyl Fetish

After touring Europe by bus in search of vintage records, two local music junkies decided to channel their passion into *Discos Paradiso*, now a fixture on lists of the world's best record stores. Since opening in 2010, it's become a temple for vinyl lovers, specializing in new and used records with a deep focus on house, techno, electro and ambient, while still covering most styles. As the epicenter of Barcelona's electronic scene, the shop doubles as a community hub for DJs and producers, hosting regular in-store events and live sets that keep the energy spinning.

• Discos Paradiso, Carrer de Ferlandina 39, El Raval, discosparadiso.com

Local Tastes

Markets are an authentic way to feel a city's heartbeat, from gray-haired neighbors trading gossip to old-timers savoring their first cerveza of the day. They're also where Catalonia's true flavors come alive. Skip *La Boqueria*'s selfie crowds and head for the markets that locals love, like *Llibertat* in Gràcia or *Santa Caterina* (photo) in El Born. In Eixample, seek out the hand-stuffed olives at *La Concepció*, or choose a fresh catch at *Medusa 73* for a laid-back lunch with hand-cut fries inside *Ninot* market.

• Various Locations

Photos: Samuel Sweet, Valeria Capri (x3), Turisme de Barcelona

Paula Errando

Indie Fashion Advocate

The monthly *Palo Market Fest* has become one of Barcelona's most anticipated creative gatherings. Held inside the renewed 19th-century Palo Alto factory in Poblenou, the market brings together a curated selection of independent designers, artisans and emerging brands. Visitors wander among fashion labels, handmade accessories and home goods, while DJs spin, food trucks serve and cocktails flow in the leafy garden courtyards. Tickets often sell out in advance, a sign of how the market has grown. Cofounder Paula Errando tells more.

Palo Market Fest
Poblenou

Levens Jewels
Gràcia

Paloma Wool
Eixample

Fundació
Joan Brossa
El Born

Sala Beckett
Poblenou

Teatre Lliure
Montjuïc

Grec Festival
de Barcelona
Montjuïc

The Heartbreak
Hotel
Sants

How did the market first come together?

My father worked for an important fashion brand with his brothers, and it suddenly had to close. At the time, there were gastronomic markets with a lot of success, and he thought we could do something similar in Palo Alto focused on the design world. We thought it would be easy, but all of the designers kept saying, "Go further, be more ambitious." When we finally opened in 2014, it was an unexpected success, with lines stretching around the building.

How has Barcelona changed since the market started

After we opened, there was a boom of fashion events like us, but most of them have closed. Maybe we just have a different appeal. We always want to feel like an old marketplace or meeting point where people come together and enjoy themselves. The city has also changed a lot. It feels like there are not as many Catalan locals anymore. We see a lot more expats, and we need to have the capacity to include them while being a friendly place for the locals.

How would you describe the types of vendors you host?

For fashion and accessories, it's usually a small brand managed by one or two people. We try to provide a solution for entrepreneurs and microbusinesses in a very fragile industry. They are usually young people concerned about the environment and focused on originality. About 30 percent are regulars, 30 percent are semi-regular, and the rest are usually new. Every vendor goes through a review process, and it's a curated selection each month where not everyone gets in. The idea is to give constancy and security to long-time vendors but surprise the attendees with new offers.

What are some of your favorite vendors?

I don't want to say "favorite," but I can say which ones are more emblematic of our values. UAP & Company, designed and produced in Catalonia by 19-year-old Pau. Palombella, which sells candles and skin cosmetics without endocrine disruptors. Monica Regincos, who has a handbag collection. Luz Negra, artistic jewelry created by Cristina. I want to buy something from Luz Negra. She's amazing.

Outside of the market, what are the best areas to shop for independent designers?

It used to be very localized, but not anymore. Many independent brands try to sell online because they can't afford a place, and those who can are usually distributed around the city. In a sense, this is nice because you can find something interesting wherever you are. That said, there are several local brands we want to have in Palo Market. *Levens Jewels*, *Paloma Wool* and ROWSE cosmetics would be amazing. There's also Kintana, D'Ars Atelier and Jordi Canudas, who have been or will soon be with us.

Aside from fashion, you're a theater director. What local theaters do you recommend?

Fundació Joan Brossa has an interesting program curated by Georgina Oliva. *Sala Beckett* is run by Toni Casares, an old-school theater man, with a young director named Anna Serrano. *Teatre Lliure* is institutional, and the *Grec Festival de Barcelona* is amazing during the summer. It's now curated by an interesting tandem of women. *The Heartbreak Hotel* is a tiny, special place in Sants. Even if you don't understand the language, theater can be interesting if you enjoy the energy, production and performances.

Digitally Loaded

Few understand digital art like Alex Simorré, founder of the audiovisual studio Artbox. Leveraging decades of expertise, he unveiled *Load Gallery* in 2024 with an extraordinary roster of talent. Start with local visionary Six N. Five, whose surreal worlds inspired collaborations with Cartier, Burberry and Tiffany & Co. Then there's Pilar Zeta, a mystical futurist in Mexico City, who's exhibited her work on the Giza Pyramids and several album covers for Coldplay, earning a Grammy nod along the way. The lineup spans continents, from Nigeria to South Korea; work from Swede Simon Rydén is pictured at right. Load Gallery is open Thursday to Saturday evenings, with free entry.

• Load Gallery, Carrer de Llull 134, Poblenou, load-gallery.com

Art & Design

Vanguards × Vaults

Look beyond the icons to uncover Barcelona's new wave of creative brilliance.

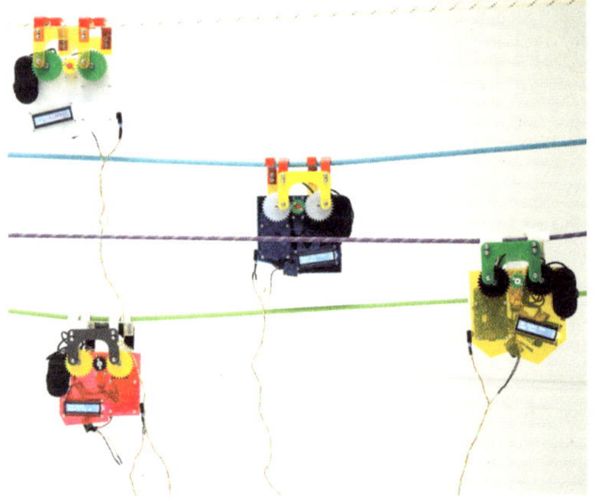

Art of the Hack

Mónica Rikić is a media artist and coder who probes the blurry boundaries between humans and machines. Her work tackles philosophical questions about artificial intelligence and digital identity through handmade robots, bespoke electronic devices and interactive installations. In one project, a "robotic micro-society" (photo) gossips about people based on their social media data, a playful yet unnerving commentary on our algorithmic lives. Though she exhibits across Europe and beyond, Rikić often showcases her installations in Barcelona, her hometown.

• Mónica Rikić, monicarikic.com

Light Layers

Onionlab creates worlds made of light. Often compared to Tokyo's teamLab, the studio crafts immersive installations and audiovisual experiences that turn architecture into canvas and light into language. Or, as the studio describes it, "Imagining tomorrow through art, design and technology." Local creators for almost 20 years, Onionlab often showcases their work in Barcelona, with installations at *LLUM BCN* and the *White Rabbit* museum in recent years.

• Onionlab, onionlab.com

Look Up

Ciutat Vella charms visitors with its crooked corners and weathered stone facades, but Carrer de Milans adds a hidden twist. Midway through the 320-foot street, the walls curve outward to form a small circular center known as Plaça de Milans. Designed in the 19th century by local architect Francesc Daniel Molina, the 15-sided space was an ingenious attempt to bring sunlight into the shadowy maze of the Old City. Yet what makes it unforgettable isn't the history, it's the perspective. Stand in the center and look up. The cornices of the buildings carve a perfect geometric ring into the sky overhead.

• Carrer de Milans, Gothic Quarter

The Last Kiss

Cemetery selfies usually mean Jim Morrison's grave in Paris. Poblenou offers something far more haunting. Founded in the 18th century as the city's first official burial ground, *Poblenou Cemetery* is a showcase of neoclassical and modernista mausoleums, but its true icon is *The Kiss of Death*. This marble masterpiece captures a winged skeleton gently kissing the forehead of a young man in rapt surrender, a chilling yet beautiful vision of mortality and grace. Morbid? Maybe. But as funerary art goes, it's hard to find a more striking work.

• Poblenou Cemetery, Avenida d'Icària 204, Poblenou

1970s Sci-Fi Studios

Completed in 1975 by architect Ricardo Bofill, *Walden 7* was a social-housing experiment inspired by the utopian ideals of the sci-fi novel *Walden Two*. The project reimagined urban life as a "City in Space," with a vertical maze of 18 interconnected towers built from modular units that can be rearranged into apartments of varying sizes. Behind its terracotta facade lies a surreal labyrinth of bridges, balconies, pools, gardens and seven-story courtyards, all designed to foster community within density. For a glimpse inside this retro-futuristic wonder, cue up the "Warts" music video by Hinds.

• Walden 7, Calle Carretera Reial 106, Sant Just Desvern, walden7.com

Jasmin Waschl

Guardian of Underground Art

Jasmin Waschl left Berlin in the early 2000s for what was becoming one of the world's most exciting underground art scenes in Barcelona. Her apartment became a gallery, eventually leading to an official space, *Fousion Gallery*, in the chicest section of El Born. The scene may have retracted as the city's global profile grew, but Jasmin continues to hold the line with artists from the original scene and emerging talent with the same street-level attitude.

What is the history of the gallery?

We started in 2005 as an apartment gallery in the historic center of Barcelona. We focused on urban art and surrealism during a time when international artists were coming here. Artists like Banksy were regularly painting the walls of Barcelona. Many of us came between 2003 and 2005 when the city became a hub for the underground scene, and not just for art. The city was a skate hub, the music scene was growing, and it was a mecca for graffiti. Within this context, we built up the apartment gallery, and then we started going to art fairs in London, Paris, New York and so on. Now we have this dedicated gallery space that opened a few years ago.

What sparked the underground scene 20 years ago? Cheaper rent in places like Poblenou?

Poblenou was full of old warehouses, often occupied [by squatters] and the underground party scene. It was one of the most important scenes for electronic music and art in Europe. A lot of people got inspired in Barcelona. At this time, it was accessible with big spaces for creation. Later on, Barcelona got more touristy, commercial, gentrified and expensive, so many artists had to leave. Sometimes we get disoriented in Poblenou because of all the new office buildings and tech companies. The scene is not gone, but the space is much more limited. Wherever there is a lot of grunge, the artist comes and takes the first step, and the next step is the inevitable hipster movement and gentrification.

Tell me about the early graffiti scene.

If we're talking about the 1990s, Barcelona started to become a graffiti hub on the underground level. You see it clean now, but back then, the city was completely bombed [with paint]. It was like a huge mural. You also had spaces in the streets or backyards or empty houses where parties just spontaneously started. The party scene was much bigger and more organic than now. The cleaning of Barcelona started in the 2000s, so if graffiti goes up one day, someone paints over it the next. The city was preparing to sell Barcelona to tourists. It felt like the slow killing of a big scene. People get older, and maybe the younger generation appreciates different things, so everything has its time. We are all happy that we experienced it, that we lived it, because it was really a special time.

If you want to find underground culture in the city now, where do you go?

You have many spots, but you have to know where, and it might be at events or street festivals. In some cases, people from the underground now work with the city on public events. For example, NEO is an association in Poblenou, and they have a stage at Fiesta Mayor del Poblenou where they promote experimental sounds and underground art. You still have the scene, but it might not exist anymore in the same organic form.

Is it true that more underground artists are moving to L'Hospitalet for cheaper rents?

Yes, but it's also because it's an industrial zone with bigger spaces. Some people have already declared it the new Brooklyn of Barcelona, and yes, the rents are cheaper, but it's also happening in a natural, organic way. It's still in the metro. It's accessible. L'Hospitalet is the second biggest city [by population] in Catalonia, but it's really just an extension of Barcelona.

What artists do you represent who were born in Barcelona?

Llia Mayer, Samuel Salcedo, Alberto de Blobs, Kenor, who was one of the first in the abstract graffiti movement. We also have legends like Miss Van who moved here from France around 2003. Victor Castillo came around the same time before moving to Los Angeles, and now he's between Chile and Barcelona again. From the pop surrealists, Dilka Bear and Mono Cieza also came to Barcelona early on.

What are the best places to see street art in Barcelona?

Graffiti or street art?

Well, not paid murals on the side of a touristy coffee shop.

I would categorize that as street art. Graffiti means it's unpaid and illegal, and the whole city is full of it. When the street shutters go down in front of all the storefronts, you'll see that many are painted. The shutters are the responsibility of the shop, not the government, so it only gets removed if the shop owners want. Still, there is a hierarchy to painting the shutters, rules that you don't cross. Some graffiti has been on shutters for 20 years. You don't paint over somebody's graffiti, though there can be exceptions depending on your level.

You have to be better and more famous?

Yes, that's the unwritten rule. It needs to be better. In the 1990s, it was a style war with graffiti crews,

Parc del Fòrum
Sant Adrià de Besòs

The Three Chimneys
Poble Sec

Alfons X
Gràcia

Petra
El Born

Bodega del Vermut
Gothic Quarter

San Pedrito
El Born

OMA
Eixample

AURELIEN
Gràcia

Fundació Joan Miró
Montjuïc

Poble Espanyol
Montjuïc

The Museu Nacional d'Art de Catalunya
Montjuïc

Teatre Grec
Montjuïc

Reial Cercle Artístic
Gothic Quarter

Barcelona Cathedral
Gothic Quarter

and it was about the spots, so there are all these unwritten rules about who has a right to paint over who. The more you're known, the possibility that you get crossed is quite low.

What's the best neighborhood for shutters?

The center is full of shops, and the industrial areas, like around *Parc del Fòrum*, have a lot of the old construction walls. They need to build a wall during construction, and it's not protected or fined because it's the owner's wall, not a public space. You have a big area around *The Three Chimneys* on Paral·lel that is legally organized and managed. The highways, railways and the trains were the original habitat for graffiti, and during the pandemic, all the trains were painted again because it couldn't be controlled. That is the nature of the proper graffiti world.

If somebody wants a photo in front of a local street mural, which one would you recommend?

One of the biggest and best is Miss Van's mural near the *Alfons X* metro station in Gracia. She painted it in 2016, and it's still in a perfect state.

Let's talk about food. What restaurants do you recommend?

Petra for fusion Catalan, and we are good friends with *Bodega del Vermut*, an authentic vermouth and tapas bodega. It's one of the best anchovies in Barcelona. *San Pedrito* for Mexican food. *OMA* is very good. *AURELIEN* makes a lot of strange ice cream.

What are some recommendations for a park or a hike?

For hiking, there's Tibidabo. It's a big natural park, luckily, which is why they cannot build any more in the Collserola [Natural Park]. This is where you get the best views over Barcelona, from everywhere. It's one of the best hiking spots where you can get lost for hours [in a good way] on the Carretera de les Aigües. It's the lung of Barcelona, and then you have the smaller lung, Montjuïc, which has a botanical garden and a castle on the top. You can see the industrial port of Barcelona from a green zone, so it's a nice contrast. You also have the *Fundació Joan Miró* museum there, and it's a nice walk to *Poble Espanyol*, *MNAC* [*The Museu Nacional d'Art de Catalunya*] and the *Teatre Grec*, which is a really nice spot in the summer because you have the concerts there.

Your choice for a city beach?

Even if it's overcrowded, I'm still a fan of Barceloneta. It's really practical when you just want to jump into the water without traveling far. If you want to go a bit outside, you could head to Ocata or take the train 20 minutes to Castelldefels. I would say go to the beach behind Fòrum. The city beaches are the most crowded from June to August, which we call the sardine box.

What is the best art fair in Barcelona?

Oh, there's no good art fair in Barcelona. Okay, for more generic art, I guess, but you have to go to Madrid to see a proper art fair. For us, the best one is Estampa, actually. ARCOmadrid as well, but it's huge. It's one of the biggest international art fairs.

How often do you host art openings?

About every two and a half months, depending on art fairs and holidays and outside shows. For example, we just did some big exhibitions in the *Reial Cercle Artístic* in front of the *Barcelona Cathedral*, and we did two shows in Mexico. Sign up for the mailing list to know when they're happening.

Poe de Laf

Wrap It Up

Poe de Laf, a Barcelona expat from Marseille, is a *Fousion Gallery* artist who wraps people in fabric materials and paints them. Joining gallery owner Jasmin Waschl during her interview, the artist answered a few questions about her work and adopted city.

How would you describe your artwork?

When I was painting, I always had this sense of meditation and wanting to go more inside. You close everything, and then when you go out, you see everything in a different way. I wanted to do something like Christo, the artist who wrapped monuments in fabrics. I was doing portraits, and I started to wrap people to find another way to find expressiveness without just a face. Now I want to wrap everything, just to see things differently. With more color, maybe.

Is there symbolism in wrapping people? For example, are they trying to hide themselves?

No, it's not about trying to hide. It's about trying to find yourself.

What inspired you to move to Barcelona from Marseille?

I was doing a PhD in art history about animals in modern art. I came here for just three months, during that time Jasmin described, and I said I can't go back. I didn't want to go back.

Art & Design

Bespoke Bathrooms

A city so elegantly cool that even your bladder gets a view.

Royal Court

A tribute to 1930s modernist glamour, the bathrooms at *El Nacional* are as photogenic as the food court itself. Designed by Lázaro Rosa-Violán, the acclaimed creative designer behind some of the world's most striking interiors, the space dazzles with dramatic lighting, marble finishes and ornate mirrors that echo the venue's Art Nouveau aesthetic.

• El Nacional, Passeig de Gràcia 24 Bis, Eixample, elnacionalbcn.com

Photos: Valeria Capri

Flipping Out

The original *Machaka* hides its bathroom behind a fridge door, but the Carrer del Consell de Cent outpost takes the concept to another level. Here, a disguised shelving unit opens into a fluorescent fever dream that resembles a crime scene under blacklight. Liquid soap oozes from ketchup and mustard dispensers, a cross-dressing mannequin hangs from the ceiling and neon-splattered walls welcome your graffiti scribble.

• Machaka, Carrer del Consell de Cent 421, Eixample, machakaburger.es

Mirror Ball

"Let's put a disco in the bathroom." One can only imagine the planning meeting where that idea was hatched, but *Boca Grande* couldn't have hoped for a better outcome. Beneath the polished restaurant, the basement bathroom (shared with sister bar *Boca Chica*) shimmers with a mosaic of mismatched mirrors, but it's the impromptu dance parties that made it legendary. DJs rock the space Thursday to Saturday nights.

• Boca Grande, Passatge de la Concepció 12, Eixample, bocagrande.cat

Photos: Ignacio Vinyas @ignaciovinyas_

Private Party

You wouldn't expect a venue that's hosted Post Malone and Lucien Laviscount to greet guests with a decorative sink and urinals, but *Chica Club* loves a good twist. The cheeky nod to its neighbor and muse, *Boca Grande*, sets the tone for what follows: a sleek, star-powered space built around big-name DJs, top-tier cocktails and a strict no-photos policy. Entry is by reservation only, with the evening warming up at 10pm in the cocktail bar before the club gets lit at midnight.

• Chica Club, Carrer del Rosselló 217, Eixample, chicabcn.cat

Spain's First Influencers

Photo: Elsa Peretti en Boccacio. Barcelona, 1967 © Archivo Colita Fotografía

Gauche Divine and the Bocaccio Nightclub

A photo showcase by Colita and Oriol Maspons

In 1967, a new discotheque on Carrer de Muntaner became headquarters for a revolution. Not the violent kind Franco's regime feared, but something perhaps more dangerous: posh progressives partying their way toward freedom.

Bocaccio was ground zero for the Gauche Divine (literally "Divine Left"), an influential circle of wealthy youth interested in pop culture, fashion and visual arts. The name, coined by writer Joan de Sagarra in 1969, was meant to mock the contradiction: left-wing intellectuals from Barcelona's haute bourgeoisie, sipping whisky and discussing Marx in designer clothes. But the group embraced the irony, turning it into their banner.

The Gauche Divine showed little interest in traditional Spanish politics. Perhaps genuine indifference, perhaps strategic cover. Either way, they understood something fundamental: Culture changes before politics does. Their weapon was lifestyle.

In this final decade of the Franco regime, Spain felt the squeeze of cultural restrictions, media censorship and repressive social codes. The Gauche Divine embodied the opposite—avant-garde culture, cosmopolitan attitudes and sexual liberation—and they spread their counterculture influence through books, films, photography and the *Bocaccio* magazine and music label.

The nightclub was the physical manifestation of these values. Owner Oriol Regàs (pictured on the next page) had already made his name with *Via Veneto*, one of Salvador Dalí's favorite restaurants. The Bocaccio's inauguration, which the surrealist icon attended, set the tone with American music like the Beach Boys' "Good Vibrations" and the Mamas and the Papas' "Monday, Monday." Frowned upon by the Church, this music wasn't widely available in Spain, so the Gauche Divine brought it back, along with modern fashion, from regular trips to London and Paris.

Bocaccio also became a runway for fashion styles. Oriol Maspons' photo on the opposite page captures one such event, but the Mary Quant fashion show might have been the most legendary. Quant, herself part of the Swinging Sixties scene in London, is widely credited with creating the modern miniskirt. Spanish society might've viewed her creation as morally corrupting, but inside the club that night, London models in miniskirts were dancing barefoot to the Beatles. Photographers captured this celebration of modernity and defiance, and the images became iconic symbols of cultural liberation.

Some critics dismissed the group as wealthy dilettantes who partied while real dissidents risked prison. Yet it raises the question of which tactic sparked deeper change. What they lacked in ideological purity, they made up for in cultural permission, showing ordinary Spaniards that they, too, could be modern, successful and free.

For the Gauche Divine, the most subversive act was showing a repressed society what it was missing. They became Barcelona's beautiful resistance, proving that sometimes the most dangerous rebels march in designer shoes.

Photo: Oriol Regàs y gogós. Barcelona, 1968 © Archivo Colita Fotografía

IKE DANC

Showcase

Legacy

The 2020 exhibition *Bocaccio: El Temple de la Gauche Divine* celebrated the club's legacy, with local studio Run Design recreating its original look and feel, surrounding visitors with photographs, magazines and other artifacts from its glamorous heyday.

Flash Flash, one of the few surviving haunts of the Gauche Divine, has kept its doors open for more than 55 years. Its white walls are lined with playful black-and-white portraits of photographer Karin Leiz captured by Leopoldo Pomes, both central figures in the creative circle. Another member, Colita, shot a now-iconic image of Bocaccio founder Oriol Regàs within these same walls.

The Local Plate

Where innovation challenges tradition, and both come out stronger.

Critics Choice

No existing tapas restaurant in Barcelona has climbed higher on the world's best restaurants list than *Cal Pep*, a neighborhood institution since 1989. With no fixed menu, the restaurant relies on waiters to guide the experience, but signature dishes like Spanish tortilla and botifarra sausage stuffed with foie gras are unmissable. Smaller groups must queue for counter seats at the bar, the perfect vantage point to watch the team work its magic. Parties of four or more can reserve a table in the back for a more relaxed experience.

• Cal Pep, Plaça de les Olles 8, El Born, calpep.com

Market Place

Serving just eight diners daily, *Olivos Comida y Vinos* is as intimate as it gets. Chef Ezequiel Devoto crafts tasting menus inspired by the morning's market finds, while his wife, María, curates a warm, living-room atmosphere and thoughtful wine list. Recognized by Michelin, Repsol and the Slow Food Guide, the restaurant offers a standard tasting menu for €90 and a pre-ordered Inspiration Menu for €110 to €120. Typically open for lunch only, with dinner on Fridays, Olivos has a little-known secret: private Inspiration Menu dinners for four to six guests. There's no surcharge for exclusivity, but reservations need to be made a week or more in advance.

• Olivos Comida y Vinos, Carrer de Galileu 159, Sants, olivoscomidayvinos.com

Catalan Classic

Born from a local blog, *Morro Fi* champions authentic Catalan culture and ignited the city's vermouth revival. At the original Consell de Cent location, the menu is handwritten in Catalan across white-tiled walls, lending a no-nonsense local charm. Start with a glass of house-made vermouth over ice, garnished with an olive, then dive into a classic gilda skewer (anchovy, olive and piparra pepper) or *gruesas y mejillones* (crispy potato chips layered with mussels, olives and house sauce). For round two, just point at whatever catches your eye behind the counter. Morro Fi now has five locations, with cooked-to-order options at the L'Illa Diagonal food court.

• Morro Fi, several locations, morrofi.cat

Shovel & Share

Street Fish made its name with one bold move: serving seafood on a shovel. Not on ice or a fancy platter, but a real metal shovel piled high with treasures from the sea. For €18 per person, it arrives loaded with mussels, clams, razor clams, squid, shrimp, a local scallop and an amazing social media opportunity to record. Want to go bigger? Upgrade with grilled crayfish or a whole lobster. It's a fun, no-frills seafood feast that's designed to share.

• Street Fish, Carrer de Nicaragua 140, Les Corts, street-fish.es

Photos: Cal Pep, Olivos, Morri Fi, Street Fish

Toni Varela

No Rules, No Limits

Casa Varela 1986, a family-run fixture in L'Hospitalet de Llobregat, was on the brink. Unsure how much longer the restaurant could survive, son Toni Varela stepped in, not to steady the ship but to risk it all on dramatic change. Rather than cling to a fading formula, Toni reinvented the restaurant as a free-thinking modern kitchen that deserves to spearhead a new wave of Catalan cuisine. A bold claim? Absolutely. But Toni's a bold chef. He's the type who tops steak-and-eel tartare with mustard-truffle ice cream, a combination that shouldn't possibly work but emerged as a bestselling signature dish. Backed by a first-class team, Toni has introduced a new Casa Varela, ready to rock for another 40 years.

How would you describe Casa Varela to someone who has never been here?

It's like coming to a family home, to my house. It's a warm, friendly atmosphere with refined service but without too much formality. I really like Italian trattorias, the energy, the closeness, like you're welcoming family, which is how we treat people. That's why it's called Casa Varela.

The restaurant takes traditional Spanish dishes and gives them a creative twist. What dish best represents tradition and creativity at the same time?

That's the key, that's what I try to do with my team, to give dishes that special touch to make them different from others. For me, it would be the tripe with smoked octopus, where I combine my taste for Asian food with Spanish tradition. Or the black angus paella with black Manchurian mushrooms, which we make with shiitake and mirin mushrooms and sake. We combine Mexican flavors, which I love, with Galician pork knuckle to make tacos. There are many types of croquette, but we make oxtail croquettes with prawn tartare. There are lots of Iberian pork dishes, but we make ours with Chinese noodles and hoisin sauce. Then there's the cheek cannelloni with gorgonzola cream. In the end, it's about turning your brain around and finding different ways to make a dish.

The restaurant opened almost 40 years ago. How was Casa Varela back then?

My mother was a fishmonger in a fish shop, and my father founded the restaurant with his sister. It started as a Galician food bar, and then they moved on to the menu. My aunt left because she had to take care of her family, and my mother came in and started creating a daily menu. The restaurant did well until the financial crisis hit, and then it started to decline. I arrived in 2011 and created a new menu with [chef] Jordi. By 2021, we were doing so well that we could make renovations and pay off our debt.

Did your mom have the same creative style?

No, my mother was super traditional. In fact, the chicken croquettes and rice are still made the same way. Mixing ham with clams, my father's Galician food, everything is from them. I am who I am thanks to them. I have been able to see the good and the bad, and I've tried to keep the good. They were my school. I always say that she was a diamond in the rough because no one cooks like she does. If she had the vision we have now, my mother would've been one of the best cooks in Catalonia, but in those days, it was a different world.

Casa Varela 1986
L'Hospitalet de Llobregat

Bar Córdoba
L'Hospitalet de Llobregat

Eldelmar
La Vila Olímpica del Poblenou

Cocina Hermanos Torres
Les Corts

La Boqueria
Gothic Quarter

She must be proud of what is happening now.

Yes, very much so.

What is the most important thing you learned about your mother's cooking?

Love for the person. Cooking for people as if they were your own mother. Putting all your love into it. That's what I learned from her.

What less common Spanish wine would you recommend to someone visiting?

The Canary Islands are doing some really cool stuff, but the king of it all is Raúl Pérez, who is doing incredible things with mencía [grapes] in Galicia. He has a 100-point wine in Robert Parker. It's a €600 bottle, very top-notch.

What about a bottle for under €50?

Raza from Carmelo Rodero. We have it here. It's very good.

Where do you go for traditional tapas?

Bar Córdoba in Hospitalet is traditional, pure and simple. He's my friend, and he's been there for many years. It's very emblematic of Hospitalet.

What local experiences do you recommend for people visiting Barcelona?

Eating paella by the sea in an area other than the city center. There's the new restaurant at the Olympic Port, *Eldelmar*, from [three-Michelin starred] *Hermanos Torres*. Sitting on that terrace with the sea, good seafood, good company, good wine . . . for me, that would be a great experience. There aren't many options by the sea from Barcelona to Sitges, but there are tons of great places from Mataró north. In fact, my cuisine is very similar to that of Empordà in the Girona area [to the north]. I like it a lot.

What about the neighborhood mercats?

I know it's touristy, but you have to see *La Boqueria*. I'd also recommend Caterina and Sant Antoni, but every market has its charm. When I go to other countries, I always go to the markets, especially in Italy. The ones I liked the most were in Florence, Venice and Verona.

What do you consider the current restaurant trends in Barcelona?

It's this "Barcelona hippie" style where the chefs create a place with maybe a [Josper] charcoal oven and a very balanced cuisine. I don't know what to call it, if "hippie" is the right word, but it's a freer technique. Starting in a tiny place with nothing and just creating, like in the television series *The Bear*. That's the change in haute cuisine, how I see it, and it's very creative. It's very good. The restaurants are top-notch, run by young chefs who are starting to do amazing things.

You've had offers to open another restaurant. What's the latest?

We've been offered cities like Madrid and Miami, but I see it as far away in the end. I don't know what will come. I did go to Dubai because I was very interested in seeing it, but I realized it wasn't for me. Everything felt cold. I have my investor, my financial godfather, and he's my top guy. Hopefully I can open something with him one day because he's like family. He wants me to go to Miami, and you never know, because loyalty for me is everything.

Latin America × Barcelona

More than a third of Barcelona residents were born outside of Spain, with more than half arriving from Latin America. Chefs from these countries have made the city a stage to refine and elevate their culinary traditions, often blending them with European techniques and ingredients. For instance, the collaboration between Peruvian and Japanese cuisine has found high-end expressions in Barcelona.

"We take the Peruvian and the Japanese traditions and try to improve them with the ingredients we have here," says Jorge Muñoz, who ran the Michelin-starred *Pakta* in Poble Sec before returning to Lima as head chef at *Astrid y Gastón*. "Peru and Japan don't have black truffles, but we have them in Spain, so we need to find a dish where we can combine all the ingredients: the citrus, the spicy, the black truffle."

Mexico City–born Paco Méndez, one of the first chefs in Europe to earn a Michelin star for Mexican cuisine, earned another for his new restaurant *COME*. Now a long-time local, he remains driven to elevate his cuisine: "I'm not just serving food, I'm serving culture as well. I understand how bad Mexican cuisine has been treated [in Spain], and I want to make it right."

These acclaimed chefs are the pinnacle of a broader trend: Latin American culinary talent continues to thrive in Barcelona. We spoke with three of the city's finest to explore how they adapt their native cuisines using Spanish ingredients and techniques.

Colombia: Muysca

When it comes to Colombian cuisine, *Muysca* is unrivaled in Barcelona, perhaps all of Spain. Chefs Johnattan Arias and Camila Coronado fuse tradition and innovation, transforming classic comfort foods into elegant culinary journeys. Imagine *sobrebarriga a la brasa*, a tender flank steak, paired with cheesy *papas chorreadas* potatoes, or a beefy *posta negra cartagenera* in a panela–sweet red wine reduction. And the chicharrón? Crispy, golden, melt-in-your-mouth perfection that lingers in your memory long after the last bite. At Muysca, every dish tells a story: rooted in Colombian tradition, yet elevated with flair that feels entirely of the moment.

"Cooking Colombian cuisine with local ingredients is fascinating because the variety of Mediterranean produce is spectacular," says Johnattan, who spent six months at *Restaurante Martín Berasategui*, a three-Michelin-starred powerhouse in the Basque Country with a three-star sister restaurant (*Lasarte*) in Barcelona. "We also import key ingredients directly from Colombia, like *papas criollas*, which aren't available here, and give our dishes contemporary presentations. The goal is to highlight traditional flavors, something Spain does exceptionally well, creating a real connection between the two cuisines."

• Muysca, Carrer del Clot 135, El Clot, muysca.es

Peru: Pueblo Libre Taberna

At *Pueblo Libre Taberna*, chef Pablo Ortega brings the heart of Lima to Barcelona, keeping the flavors bold, familiar and soulful. Market-fresh ceviches pop with citrus and heat, creamy *causa* melts on the tongue, beef-stuffed rocoto peppers balance spice and richness, and duck in *huancaína* sauce delivers a cheesy, fiery punch. The chef brings the type of home-style cooking that locals expect in classic Lima eateries.

"Cooking Peruvian dishes in Spain has taught me that authenticity isn't just about ingredients, but about intention," says Pablo, a veteran of *Astrid y Gastón* in Lima. "I use local products, but the soul and memories of my country guide every dish. Recreating this cuisine in Barcelona has been a journey of adaptation and respect."

• Pueblo Libre Taberna, Carrer de Sepúlveda 151, Sant Antoni, pueblolibretaberna.com

Brazil: Buriti

At *Buriti*, chef Sara Lemos brings the vibrant flavors of Bahia to Barcelona. The kitchen hums with the aromas of coconut, palm oil and grilled *coalho* cheese, while *moquecas* bubble with fresh fish and seafood in fragrant, spiced broths. Hearty *feijoada* packs a comforting punch of beans and meat, and Brazilian staples like cheesy tapioca cubes and pillowy *pão de queijo* round out the feast. After opening her original Poblenou location, Sara brought her flavors to a second restaurant across from the Sant Antoni market.

"Barcelona's international culinary scene makes it easy to find tropical products like passion fruit, mango and coconut milk, which are essential ingredients on our menu," Sara explains. "Being on the Mediterranean is a huge advantage. Fruits and vegetables are grown with care and respect for the product, and there are African-origin products like palm oil and beans that are key to many dishes. It's about research, persistence and not giving up."

• Buriti, Carrer de Bilbao 18, Poblenou; Carrer del Comte Borrell 65, Sant Antoni, buriti.es

Albert Adrià

Beyond elBulli

The shadow of elBulli stretches across the entire culinary world. Even after closing in 2011, the Catalonia-based restaurant continues to flex with kitchen alum behind Noma, Disfrutar, Osteria Francescana, Gaggan, Mugaritz, El Celler de Can Roca, Alinea, Somni and minibar by José Andrés. Ferran Adrià was elBulli's head chef, but he proudly admits his brother Albert played an equally vital role, creating signature dishes like the liquid olive. Today, Albert continues that legacy with the Michelin-starred *Enigma* and as the 2025 Chef's Choice winner, an award voted on exclusively by the world's top chefs.

When a music artist creates a global hit, fans typically see all future music through the prism of that first song. You were part of the biggest culinary hit in modern history. How do you strike a balance between honoring your past and pushing forward with the future?

By trying not to repeat the same song. After doing elBulli, there was not much left [to do] in fine dining, but at a global level, it was possible. Time will tell.

Enigma encourages diners to experience the restaurant without preconceptions. How does this change the dining experience?

We understand Enigma as an open project that will modulate and modify with time. We want to explore the possibilities of understanding gastronomy, and that's why we surrounded ourselves with a space that allows us this polyvalence. The challenge is important, but we approach it with humility and hard work.

Top chefs tend to be very competitive, but. . . .

I think, in general, the attitude in the industry is changing. Relationships are more relaxed, and there's a tendency to take care of human relationships. This is one of the keys to success, and we try to promote this work psychology with the rest of the team. As we know, in the kitchen, one works a lot of hours, and it's normal that there are conflicts. Our work is to minimize them.

You are considered one of the all-time great pastry chefs. What skills do pastry chefs develop that make them better at crafting savory dishes?

In order to do pastry, it's necessary to have a lot of technique and knowledge, and in this case, the pastry [person] must have the mentality of a chef. In fact, I've always thought of myself as a cook, and now more than ever, even though I've been a pastry chef for decades. Most of the time in savory cooking, you have a main product as a starting point. It can be a vegetable, meat or fish, and it will mark the aesthetic and the conceptualization of the dish, but the possibilities in creating a dessert are infinite.

You had a lot of success after elBulli, particularly with Tickets, which had an atmosphere that recalled fun childhood memories. To what extent was this a reaction to the seriousness of modern gastronomy?

If Tickets must be remembered for something, I hope it's for how it socialized fine dining. We managed it so that people who were not interested in fine dining would lose their fear and preconceived ideas. Nowadays, there are a lot of restaurants with very similar profiles that offer fine dining in a very informal ambiance.

Your restaurants regularly appear on lists for the world's best. How much focus should a restaurant put on these types of lists?

A chef doesn't work to get prizes but to have the restaurant full. It is obvious that when you get the recognition, the restaurant gets full, but it's important to give prizes the appropriate importance, not more, and to accept your position in the game. Like it or not, these are the world references nowadays.

In the end, what stories do you want to tell through food?

To be happy and make other people happy.

Perfect Pours

The night is young, the drinks are legendary, and you know the assignment. Salut!

Craft Beer King

Manolo Baltasar, owner of *BierCaB*, is widely credited with introducing American craft beer to Spain. While managing a local frankfurter restaurant in the 1990s, the Barcelona native discovered the emerging craft scene and began importing beers from boutique breweries. Locals loved it, and Manolo quickly earned a reputation as the city's top beer sommelier. In 2013, he opened BierCaB, joined by his trusted right-hand man, Jose.

The bar features 30 taps that rotate IPAs, sours, barrel-aged stouts and more from Spain and around the world. Rare finds are part of the fun: Manolo once secured a limited IPA from Kyoto and the first imported kegs from Firestone Walker. European standouts like Stigbergets (Sweden), Fuerst Wiacek (Germany) and Catalan faves Soma and Dos Kiwis appear regularly. All of it pairs beautifully with BierCaB's cubed bravas or the under-€20 steak with beer-hops chimichurri. If you track your pours on Untappd, this is your temple, but even newcomers feel welcome. Manolo and Jose are always on hand to guide your experience.

• BierCaB, Carrer de Muntaner 55, Eixample, biercab.com

Bonding

Dry Martini is a local institution, renowned for its timeless elegance and flawless cocktails. Acquired in 1996 by mixologist Javier de las Muelas—the "Ferran Adrià of cocktails"—the bar has preserved its timeless English aesthetic since opening in 1978. Its namesake cocktail is the star, with a ticker proudly tallying more than one million martinis served to date. In a nod to Prohibition-era intrigue, the venue also hides *Speakeasy*, an intimate restaurant offering a tasting menu with cocktail pairings. More than a bar, Dry Martini is a rite of passage for cocktail lovers.

• Dry Martini, Carrer d'Aribau 162-166, Eixample, drymartiniorg.com

Vintage Vermutería

Since 1968, *Bodega del Vermut* has poured vermouth through three generations, with the grandchildren running the show for the past quarter-century. They work with a small Catalan producer to craft their house vermouth, using an ancestral recipe that follows the lunar cycles. The salted anchovies are equally legendary, best paired with a vermouth in the back room. The exposed stone walls and curated art make it feel like a cross between a wine cellar and an underground gallery. And take note: Authentic places call themselves bodegas. Anything labeled a "vermouth bar" or "wine bar" is suspect.

• Bodega del Vermut, Carrer de les Magdalenes 6, Gothic Quarter, @bodega_del_vermut

Wine Pairings

A century of curation awaits inside *Vila Viniteca*, where bespoke tasting experiences can include anything inside the shop and from the world-class wine store next door. The bilingual staff can help you navigate the treasure trove of artisan cheeses, cured meats and gourmet preserves (tins) to pair with just the right bottles. Vila Viniteca curates wine lists at many local restaurants, and that same expertise can design personalized pairings for you. Reservations, while available, typically aren't needed.

• Vila Viniteca, Carrer dels Agullers 9, El Born, vilaviniteca.es

Photos: Valeria Capri, Dry Martini, Caro Diux, Albert Orellana

Speakeasy Sips

The Real Hidden Gems

Secret doors and passwords await on a speakeasy bar hunt.

Finding Nevermore

The name of the speakeasy *Never* is a direct nod to the chilling final word of Edgar Allan Poe's "The Raven." This dark mood permeates the entire experience. You enter a seemingly ordinary bar, unaware of the magic that lies behind the mirror on the back wall. Beyond that threshold, the ambiance takes a stylistic turn with deep-red furniture, dimly lit corners and macabre decorations meant to imagine the house in the 1845 poem. The cocktail menu offers subtle yet sophisticated twists that are both approachable and innovative.

• Never, Carrer de la Cera 17, El Raval, @neverbcn

Photos: Valeria Capri, Jake Barberia

Cut but Not Dry

Disguised as a working barbershop, *Bobby's Free* embodies true speakeasy mystique. Behind its unassuming storefront lies a cocktail bar accessible only to those in the know, with entry granted via a password posted on Instagram. Inside, vintage décor, classic jazz and 1920s-dressed bartenders transport you to another era. Craft cocktails match the theatrical setting, arriving with inventive presentations like a popcorn box and a hanging lantern. Opened in 1975, Bobby's Free is polished yet unpretentious, a space where every detail contributes to the illusion of stepping back in time.

• Bobby's Free, Carrer de Pau Claris 85, Eixample, @bobbysfree

Behind the Counter

Monk conceals itself behind an unmarked grocery facade, drawing crowds for its theatrical reveal and pop culture–themed cocktails like Björk, Kubrick and others. *TheSupermercat* runs the same playbook across two locations—one in Gothic, another in Raval—both hidden behind supermarket fronts. The speakeasy aesthetic is polished, and the drinks are well executed, but the vibe feels intentionally designed for the tourist circuit. The staff at one of the bars all but confirmed this. Don't expect an authentic local haunt. Instead, embrace these tourist faves as fun stops on a speakeasy bar hunt in the Old City.

• Ciutat Vella, multiple locations

Photos: Valeria Capri

Raid the Fridge

Push through the refrigerator door of a working pastrami shop, and you'll find *Paradiso*, the bar that launched Barcelona's speakeasy obsession. Inside, sinuous curved wood panels ripple like Mediterranean waves, setting the stage for cocktails served in vessels shaped like seashells, monkey heads and human skulls. There's even a speakeasy within the speakeasy for private bookings. Tuscan bartender Giacomo Giannotti has racked up enough mixology awards to fill that pastrami fridge, leading Paradiso to No. 1 on the World's 50 Best Bars list.

• Paradiso, Carrer de Rera Palau 4, El Born, paradiso.cat

Meritxell Falgueras

Breaking the Wine Glass Ceiling

The wine world knows Meritxell Falgueras as a force. For more than two decades, the Barcelona native has accumulated top honors, including Sommelier of the Year, while upholding a profound family tradition. Her ancestral wine shop, *Celler de Gelida*, has been passed down through five generations since opening in 1895. It's a lineage so deep that her father and grandfather were literally born within its walls. Despite an exhaustive list of accolades as a columnist, teacher, TV personality and award-winning author, speaking with Meritxell reveals a dynamic energy that suggests she's just getting started.

Your sixth book on wine just came out. What's it about?

The book is an anonymous investigation into patriarchy in the wine world. Ninety percent of women in wine say they've felt it, and 74 percent say they've been the only woman at a wine tasting or event. I start the book like a biography, but then I talk about 200 professional women in the industry. I feel bad because at least 2,000 deserve to be mentioned.

What was your own experience?

I've had a lot of critics, but it was always about my physique or being blonde. I'm super prepared and good at my job, but when you're young, you believe what people say. Now I know it was more machismo than true. I have six books, two of them named best in the world at the Gourmand Awards, and I was just in Eva Longoria's *Searching for Spain* [on CNN] talking about Catalan wine.

You consult for Michelin-starred restaurants. Do you try different wines with their dishes?

No, look, my father was doing the wine list for elBulli, and those people are close friends. It could be you test things to see if they really go together, but a lot of it is mental. You know the wine's acidity and that a boletus [mushroom] or tartufo [truffle] will go with it. I love to pair wine with culture. People in the wine world say, "Oh, wine is culture," but then they talk about food and technical things. Pairing wine with theater, with fashion, with feelings, is what makes me special.

How would you pair wine with a fashion event?

People criticize me for this, saying, "You're very superficial," but if a man makes a pairing for a fútbol match, he's a genius! I work with a lot of stylists for television and with 080 Barcelona fashion week. As with fashion, wine has its *moda* [or fashion style]. Textured wines and young reds are better in the autumn. When it's hot in the summer, you need white wines, super aromatics with good acidity, to eat paella in front of the sea. In winter, you need wines with more body because it's cold and you drink them with steaks.

The common wisdom says you pair red wine with meat and white wine with fish. In what ways is it true, and in what ways is it not?

The important thing in life is to be happy. Yes, it is true that a xarel·lo with lemon acidity won't go with a steak. If you want white, maybe try a chardonnay double lees with a white meat, but you always need to drink what you want. Life is so stressful, you don't need to stress more about choosing wine. If you like rosé, okay, but better with finger food and Netflix.

What are the defining characteristics of Catalan wine in Tarragona?

Tarragona is weird because it has so many Denominaciónes de Origen. You have part of Penedes. You have Priorat, which, with Rioja, are the only two wine regions in Spain with the [highest-level] Denominación de Origen Calificada. You have Montstat, which is super trendy, because you have the *llicorella* terroir of Priorat with a quality price. You have Terra Alta, whose main grape is grenache, and the white grenache is super Mediterranean, a bit like the south of France. For wine tourists, you have all the wine cathedrals, but in Tarragona, you also have all the Roman places. In Empuriabrava, which is more Costa Brava with Denominació d'Origen Empordà, you have the Greek tradition as well.

Celler de Gelida
Sants

Gresca
Eixample

Art Laietà d'Alta Alella
Alella

Speaking of Costa Brava, what are the defining characteristics north of Barcelona?

The difference in Empordà is the Tramontana wind. It makes crazy people, and the wines are like Dalí, no? Super expressive, super crazy, super good.

What about a wine region in the Barcelona province?

You have Alella, the littlest one in Spain, where you have xarel·lo, which they call *pansa blanca*. The vines are just in front of the sea. You have a lot in Sant Sadurni [d'Anoia] between Tarragona and Barcelona, where you have the capital of cava. The rosé cava, with trepat, grenache, pinot noir, are super cool. If you compare the quality and price with champagne, it's a really good deal.

What about a fine-dining restaurant with a great wine list?

Gresca. It's delicious, and chef Rafa Peña is a super wine lover.

What about a vineyard somewhere close to Barcelona?

[Art Laietà] d'Alta Alella. It has super nice views of the sea. The winemaker, who is now the daughter, has one of the world's best techniques, for natural wines as well. They make spectacular cavas and have a lot of wine bar activities there. It's close to Barcelona, but it's outside the craziness of the city.

What is a lesser-known wine grape you recommend in Spain?

Xarel·lo, one of the base grapes of cava, has a lot of structure with acidity. It's super good with sushi and *coca de recapte*, a Catalan dish. Also, grenache blanca. It's not as aromatic, but it has a super nice structure in the mouth. For me, in 2026, we will talk much more about texture, about the nose of wines. Garraf, very close to Sitges, is important for red wines of *ull de llebre*, the Catalan name for tempranillo.

What bottles would you recommend in your wine store at €10, €20 and €40 price points?

In that order of price, I'd recommend Huguet de Can Feixes' Blanc Selecció, Clos Figueras' Serras del Priorat and Aalto from Bodegas Aalto.

ESCOLA EL MIRACLE

A Roman Holiday in Spain

When Caesar Augustus came to oversee military campaigns in Spain, he chose Tarragona as his base. The first Roman emperor recognized what Julius Caesar had already established: Rome's most splendid Spanish stronghold, a city protected by more than two miles of fortified walls.

This golden age unfolded 2,000 years ago, when the Iberian Peninsula was known as Hispania and this Mediterranean seaport as Tárraco. The city predates Barcelona by centuries, a powerful reminder that this region existed longer as a Roman province than as part of Spain. Its Roman legacy endures in UNESCO World Heritage sites like the seaside amphitheater, remnants of the Forum, ancient rampart walkways, the sprawling Roman Circus and a medieval cathedral built atop the foundations of a Roman temple.

The city's geography is as historic as its ruins. Rising sharply from the sea, the steep terrain served as a natural fortress for this ancient military port. Today, that topography creates a city of two distinct levels. At the base, the beach gives way to a marina lined with seafood restaurants where the day's catch arrives straight from the boats. Above, the old quarter sits perched on the hillside, its narrow streets weaving between medieval architecture and old Roman walls, all bathed in the glow of evening lights. The best way to experience this historic quarter is the way locals do: hopping between bars to sip on local wines and vermouth.

Thanks to Russian River Brewing, many people associate Pliny the Elder with beer, but the Roman naturalist was history's first recognized wine critic. Nearly two millennia ago, he wrote, "[The vineyards of] Tárraco . . . are esteemed for the choice qualities of their wine." His assessment proved prophetic, as Tarragona became the center of Spanish wine production for years.

The province produces distinctive wines from grenache and carinenya for reds and macabeu and xarel·lo for whites, among others. The most acclaimed region is Priorat, with its bold, mineral-driven reds, while Montsant wraps around Priorat like a horseshoe, offering similar intensity at gentler prices. The high-elevation vineyards of Terra Alta yield morenillo, a local grape variety that echoes the elegance of pinot noir, while Penedès reigns as the sparkling wine capital of Spain.

Beyond its wine and architecture, Tarragona anchors the Costa Dorada, or "Golden Coast," named for its soft, golden sand. Mountains to the north shelter the beaches from wind, creating calm waters that slope gently into the Mediterranean. Platja del Miracle (Miracle Beach) unfolds directly northeast of the train station, but the coastline reveals more secluded stretches tucked between rock formations that jut into the sea. About 15 minutes by car, Tamarit Beach includes views of an 11th-century castle sitting just above the waves.

Getting to Tarragona is straightforward. Regional trains from Barcelona Sants reach the Tarragona station in about 75 minutes. Fast trains cut the journey to 30 minutes but arrive at Camp de Tarragona, which sits outside the city and requires a 20-minute taxi ride to reach the center. For most visitors, the extra time on the regional train is worth the convenience of arriving in the heart of the action.

Photo: Tarragona Turisme

Editors' Picks

Made in Barcelona

Lights Out

Barcelona-born Jordi Canudas is celebrated for his industrial design, with pieces in the MoMA collection in New York. While his Dipping Light has become a modern classic, the Less Lamp is pure experimentation: a one-of-a-kind fixture meant to be finished by its owner. Using the small hammer included, you literally break the outer shell to let the light escape. Make small holes or break it in half. No two lamps will be alike.

• Less Lamp, jordicanudas.com

Modern Vermouth

If exploring local bottles to take home, bring the vermouth that fueled Barcelona's aperitif revival. *Morro Fi* serves it alongside olives, chips and other goodies, with white, red and reserva options available to go.

• Vermouth, morrofi.cat

Read

Joan Colom: Les Gens Du Raval
• Joan Colom, 2006

The Barcelona-born photographer brought his camera to Raval every weekend in the wild and dangerous 1950s, capturing the experience with intimate observations in black and white.

Barça: A People's Passion
• Jimmy Burns, 2000

More than just a fútbol club, FC Barcelona is a social phenomenon, and Jimmy Burns' book about the team (updated in 2016) captures more than 125 years of Catalan pride.

An Olympic Death
• Manuel Vázquez Montalbán, 1994

A fine example of European noir, this addition in the Pepe Carvalho series finds the detective drinking, eating, fighting and romancing during the unstable times of the 1992 Olympics.

Homage to Catalonia
• George Orwell, 1938

Years before writing his seminal classics, British writer George Orwell moved to Barcelona and fought in the Spanish Civil War, recounting the experience in his final non-fiction book.

Watch

[REC]
• Jaume Balagueró & Paco Plaza, 2007

Barcelona becomes a nightmare in this found-footage horror hit, which was followed by several sequels. The actors' genuine terror comes from never knowing what's coming next.

All About My Mother
• Pedro Almodóvar, 1999

This Oscar-winning comedic drama showcases everything that made the director famous: a stellar cast (Penélope Cruz), a labyrinthine plot and sets bursting with vibrant colors and art.

Biutiful
• Alejandro González Iñárritu, 2010

Javier Bardem earned Best Actor at Cannes for his gripping turn as a single father managing a Chinese sweatshop and contending with Senegalese street vendors hawking his goods.

Spin

"Mediterráneo"
• Joan Manuel Serrat, 1971

Joan Manuel Serrat has been a global music star since the 1960s, but he's a Catalan hero for performing in his native language under Franco, a defiance that ultimately forced him into exile until the regime ended.

"To the Funk" (Manuel De La Mare Remix)
• Lexlay, 2025

Barcelona-based DJ Lexlay has performed in 50+ countries over two decades, founding the Happy Techno label along the way. Known for blending sounds, he adds a funky bassline to this remixed Tech House track.

"El Tranvía"
• Los Sirex, 1965

In the 1960s, rock music rattled conservative Spain, and few bands embodied that spirit like Los Sirex, the local group chosen to open for The Beatles during their only Barcelona concert.

"Si No Es Hoy Cuándo Es"
• Dame Area, 2024

Catalan-Italian duo Dame Area delivers dancefloor-ready, confrontational experiences like "Si No Es Hoy Cuándo Es" that hold it down for the modern post-punk underground.

Observations

The Porter

for Francisco González Ledesma

Photo: Joao Cabral

"Manager of hydroelectric company disappears." H. F. P., the financial vice president of ENHER, went missing from his family home on Christmas Eve. The search has been complicated by the heavy snowfall in Barcelona, which has left Sant Esteve unrecognizable. The director is described as being 1.50 meters tall, 57 kilos, dark-skinned with a black moustache, and was wearing a dark suit, dark gray coat and bowler hat at the time of his disappearance. It is well known that H. F. P. has been the staunchest advocate of building a skyscraper on the site of the old Hotel Fuster. —*LA VANGUARDIA*, DECEMBER 27, 1962

Like a spot of dirt in the snow, two tiles at the entrance of Hotel Casa Fuster had spent half a century bothering people. It all began on Christmas 1962, the year a massive snowstorm ravaged the city. The hotel attributed the accident to an unforgivable oversight, an example of indecent clumsiness. A laborer dropped a pallet of potted poinsettias intended for New Year's Eve.

Casa Fuster built its entire facade with the highest-quality white marble from Carrera, a first in Barcelona. The floor was waxed with care every day, polished to look like a mirror, so much so that the reflection sometimes made people feel dizzy. But nobody told this to the laborer who moved the pallet to the ballrooms. So the man slipped, stumbled with the wooden tables and scattered the hotel entrance with pot shards. Two irreplaceable tiles, there for 40 years, were shattered. All for a few poinsettias that would not even last a month.

It happened at dawn. There were no witnesses to the incident. At least, that was the story given to the papers by the new owners of the building: National Hidroeléctrica Company of Ribagorçana (ENHER). It was like adding vinegar to a paper cut, as word had already spread that ENHER wanted to sell the Fuster to erect a skyscraper. Passeig de Gràcia, the neighborhood and the entire city had been walking around sharpening knives for months. So anger turned into confusion, and when the hotel manager tried to explain, he failed to convince anyone.

Worse still, nobody kicked out Albert Agramunt, the self-confessed marble slayer. Rather than get thrown into the street, he was offered the post of porter for life. A bloke who had nothing to do with the hotel business, known only for hanging around at the Barcelona dock and for maybe doing prison time in Sicily.

Faced with criticism, ENHER's director argued that, far from being a reward, this was the worst punishment imaginable. It would be shame taken to infinity. There, Agramunt would face repulsion for his awkwardness in future generations of guests and visitors. He would have to endure the embarrassment of feeling glared at day after day by locals and foreigners. And to make matters worse, he would never be able to remove that oppressive uniform—rain or shine, dictatorship or democracy—not even if Barça won five consecutive cups.

But that wasn't what the vigilante's expression said. Fifty years later, there was no hesitation in his eyes. There was no shame in his mouth. His hands never begged forgiveness for the heresy committed against the floor. Every Christmas Eve, the smell of myrrh sprouted from these two tiles, and the porter at Casa Fuster just smiled. With his gold-edged uniform buttoned to the neck and royal purple boots.

José Luis Correa is a professor and award-winning writer and novelist. His acclaimed crime series, which follows the exploits of detective Ricardo Blanco, celebrated its 15th novel in 2025 with The Cognac Drinker.